Welcome.

An anti joke is a type of joke in which the user is set up to expect a typical punch line, however the joke ends with such an anticlimax that it has a humor all its own.

The lack of a punch line is in fact the punch line.

Enjoy this collection of the most popular Anti Jokes submitted to the website www.anti-joke.com.

A man walks into a bar, he is an alcoholic and is ruining his family.

An Irishman walks out of a bar.

What did Stephen Hawking say to the prostitute?

My illness prevents me from achieving an erection.

Knock, Knock.

Who's there?

To.

To who?

To whom.

What is red and smells like blue paint?

Red paint.

Roses are red.
Violets are blue.
I have a gun.
Get in the van.

What’s green and has wheels?

Grass, I lied about the wheels.

How do you confuse a blond?

Paint yourself green and throw forks at her.

What’s sad about 4 black people in a Cadillac going over a cliff?

They were my friends.

There's an Irishman, a homosexual, and a Jew standing at a bar. What a fine example of an integrated community.

Why was six afraid of seven?

It wasn't. Numbers are not sentient and thus incapable of feeling fear.

Your friend is so gay he has consensual sex with other men and enjoys it.

Knock, Knock.

Who's there?

Dave.

Dave who?

Dave proceeds to break into tears as his grandmother's Alzheimer’s has progressed to the point where she can no longer remember him.

A horse walked into a bar. Several people got up and left as they spotted the potential danger in the situation.

Your momma's so fat that she should probably be worried about the increased risk of cardiovascular disease.

What's worse than finding a worm in your apple?

The Holocaust.

Why can't Michael J Fox draw a perfect circle?

Because drawing a perfect circle is impossible for any human.

A duck walks into a bar. Animal control is promptly called and the duck is released in a nearby park.

What do you call a man with no arms and no legs water skiing?

I don't know, but that sounds like a highly improbable circumstance.

A horse walks into a bar and the bartender asks "why the long face?" The horse replies "My wife is dying of cancer."

A duck walks into a over 7-11 and says "Give me some lip balm, put it on my bill!" But the cash register attendee doesn't speak English and cannot understand him. He does, however, question whether his God is punishing him because as all people know, Ducks cannot speak, however, this hallucination must be punishment for a horrid misdeed. The employee breaks down into tears and begins reciting prayer. The duck, slightly miffed, walks out, pondering why he'd need lip balm anyway, since he has no lips.

How do you wake up Lady Gaga?

You set an alarm for a reasonable hour.

Have you seen Stevie Wonder's new house?

No.

Well, it's really nice.

Two cows are in a field. Suddenly, from behind a bush, a rabbit leaps out and runs away. One cow looks around a bit, eats some grass and then wanders off.

What do you tell a woman with two black eyes?

Domestic violence is a crime. She should leave her abusive partner and seek help.

Why did the blond get fired from the M&M factory?

Repeated absences and stealing.

Your mom is so ugly that she often finds it difficult attracting members of the opposite sex.

There was a man from Dundee.
Whose limericks always ended on line three.
I don't know why.

Four blondes are driving to Disneyworld. They finally get to Florida and they see a sign that says "Disneyworld: left" so they take the left and have a wonderful time at what many people believe to be the most magical place on Earth.

Roses are red, violets are blue
I've got Alzheimer's
cheese on toast

A platypus walks into a bar. They are the only mammals with the ability to lay an egg.

A dyslexic man walked into a bar, ordered a beer, and no one was aware of his affliction.

How many Jew does it take to change a light bulb?

A light bulb cannot be changed, it either is or isn't. Do you mean replace a burned-out bulb with a new one? With design, logistics, manufacturing, marketing of just that single bulb there are many people involved. It could be argued that we all play some small part in the process.

Why are black people so good at basketball?

Dedication and hard work.

What did Batman say to Robin before they got in the car?

"Get in the car."

Two men are sitting in a pub.

One man turns to the other and says: "Last night I saw lots of strange men coming in and out of your wife's house." The other man replies:

"Yes, she has become a prostitute to subsidize her drug habit."

Why did the chicken cross the road?

The farmer left the fence open, so it wandered around and happened to cross a road.

An owl and a squirrel are sitting in a tree, watching a farmer go by. The owl turns to the squirrel and says nothing because owls can't talk.

The owl then eats the squirrel because it's a bird of prey.

What's the difference between a mountain goat and a pitching wedge?

A lot.

Did you hear about the blonde who jumped out off a bridge?

She was clinically depressed and took her own life because of her terribly low self-esteem.

What do you call a black man flying a plane?

A pilot.

Darth Vader: Luke, I am your father.
Luke: Nooooo!
Darth Vader: Yes.

If olive oil is made from olives and vegetable oil from vegetables, what is baby oil made of?

Mineral Oil, Aloe Vera Extract, Vitamin E, Acetate, Fragrance.

Why do women fake orgasms?

Because they want to give men the impression that they have climaxed.

What was Anne Frank's favorite hiding spot?

She only had one, so she was unable to pick a favorite.

What did the farmer say when he lost his tractor?

"Where's my tractor?"

How many Jews can you fit in a Volkswagen?

5 comfortably.

What did the catholic priest say to the little boy?

Nothing sexual, that kind of behavior isn't as widespread as people think.

What has 9 legs, 4 feet and is orange?

Nothing.

How many black people does it take to change a light bulb?

One, possibly two if the light bulb is high up and someone has to hold the ladder.

What do you call a black guy who is selling drugs?

A pharmacist.

How do you know when a Frenchman has been near your house?

You don't, really, unless you were there to see him or if one of your neighbors saw him. I wouldn't worry about it, really.

What do you call an anorexic with a yeast infection?

A girl who really needs to see the doctor.

What’s brown and sticky?

A stick.

Why did the straight man turn gay?

He didn't. He was always gay but had to hide this from his family and friends because of an overwhelming sense of homophobia in his community.

How do two porcupines make love?

It's doubtful porcupines feel higher emotions like love. They simply mate for reproductive purposes.

What would George Washington do if he were alive today?

Scream and scratch at the top of his coffin.

What's red and invisible?

No tomatoes.

A bear walks into a bar.

Confused and disoriented it attacks several patrons.

What’s a cannibals favorite game?

Monopoly but on occasion Chutes and Ladders.

What’s red and hurts your teeth?

A brick.

What did the homeless man get for Christmas?

Nothing.

What do you get when you put a baby in a blender?

A life sentence.

How do you make a plumber cry?

Kill his family.

What would you call the Flintstones if they were all black?

A more accurate representation of the Stone Age.

What do you call an Alzheimer's patient eating?

To get to the other side.

What's the square root of 69?

8.30662386

What is the difference between Sarah Palin's mouth and Vagina?

Her mouth is for food and her vagina is for reproduction.

Knock, Knock

Who's there?

You're delusional and paranoid. Just open the door.

Why did the Catholic priest get sent to prison?

Tax evasion.

If April showers bring May flowers, what do may flowers bring?

Airborne allergens that cause millions of people to suffer everyday.

A plan with 12 passengers crashes into a cemetery. 200 bodies are found at the scene.

The horror.

Classic joke setup.

Rational explanation of that joke.

A blonde and brunette are shipwrecked on a desert island.

The eventually died of exposure.

What’s yellow and points north?

If it was possible, a magnetic banana.

A bear walks into a bar and orders a drink. The bartender knows that bears can't talk and realizes he must be dreaming. He wakes up and rolls over to tell his wife about the dream. She hears the joke, but turns away from him and pretends to be asleep. Then the bartender begins to cry. His marriage is in shambles.

Why don't Polish girls swim in the sea?

The only sea that Poland borders on is the Baltic. Throughout most of the year this sea is too cold to comfortably swim in.

What's green and fluffy?

Red fluff, if you're color blind.

A man is stranded on a deserted island with no food, water or clothing and he comes upon a magical genie lamp, a genie pops out and tells him that he has three wishes, the man asks for food, water, and clothing, the genie says "of course" the man was elated but then the genie says "but I'm afraid to tell you that genies don't exist and your hallucinating from your harsh living conditions...I'm sorry". The man lived two more weeks before dying slowly.

What's the longest, hardest thing on a black man?

His femur.

Why didn't Hitler drink whiskey?

Because it made him mean.

How was copper wire invented?

Probably some scientist did that.

A man walks into the local grocery store on his way to work. He stops by the pastry section to buy a bagel. As he is paying, the cashier says "and here's some blueberries, they're complimentary." The man looks at the blueberries expectantly. When they don't say anything he looks up, feeling foolish and pays for his bagel then heads off to work as a partner in a lawyer firm.

Why don't blondes wear watches?

In the technologically advanced age that we live in, the watch is rapidly being replaced with other electronic devices that tell time, such as cell phones or iPods.

What's red, blue, green, yellow, pink, purple, orange, teal, light green, brown, black and white?

Colors, except for black and white, for they are the absence and amalgam of all colors, respectively.

What do you call a boomerang that doesn't come back when you throw it?

A stick.

I'm on the sea food diet.

A large proportion of my daily food intake consists of fish.

What did Helen Keller say to a stranger at a party?

I earned a Bachelor of Arts degree, wrote several books, traveled to over 39 countries, and was awarded the Presidential Medal of Freedom, one of the United States' highest two civilian honors, from President Lyndon B. Johnson.

What’s the quickest way to a woman's heart?

A bilateral incision on the upper left region of the sternum.

A man is walking on the beach and discovers a lamp in the sand. He takes it home to polish it. Eventually it looks like new and he gets a fairly reasonable price from an antique shop.

A man walks into a bar and orders six shots.
The bartender asks, "Rough day?"
The man replies, "Yes, very rough."
The man later went home and hung himself.

Abe Lincoln, George Washington, George Bush and Barack Obama are sitting at a table at a bar.

They discuss politics and time travel.

Two muffins are in an oven. Although they both possess the extraordinary ability to speak, strangely each remains silent, apparently lost in their own thoughts. Thus nobody has any reason to think they are any different than any other muffins. Later after they've been baked and allowed to cool, they are sold to a woman who eats them along with a small salad. She enjoys their chewy, hearty texture, and lightly sweet taste. She is completely unaware of what amazing discovery has just been lost to science.

Three blondes were walking through the forest when they came upon a set of tracks.

The first blonde said, "Those are deer tracks."
The second blonde said, "No, those are elk tracks."
The third blonde said, "You're both wrong, those are moose tracks."

They were moose tracks.

Jim and Larry work together. Jim works hard, and Larry is a bit of a prankster.

One day, Jim is having a rather rough day, and Larry looks to cheer him up with a good-natured joke. Knowing that Jim's wife prepares dinner for him every night of the week, he calls her and tells her that their boss has decided to pay for a dinner out, that she should take the day off and just get ready for Jim to come home and pick her up. Larry will later follow up by calling a pizza delivery place and have them send a special no hard feeling message with two large delicious pizzas.

He forgets to call the pizza delivery man until later that night, after which it's too late and he thinks "I'll just explain the joke to Jim tomorrow." And goes peacefully to sleep.

Arriving home and finding that dinner is not prepared, Jim savagely beats his wife.

Why did the chicken cross the road?

To get to the other side.

Thanks!

This book is dedicated to the Internet.

We are deeply grateful to all the users of anti-joke.com who submitted the anti jokes included in this book.

To view and participate with all of our sites please visit:

horseheadhuffer.com

2622103R00052

Printed in Great Britain
by Amazon.co.uk, Ltd.,
Marston Gate.